Leaving Tracks:
A Prairie Guide

poems by

Sarah Fawn Montgomery

Finishing Line Press
Georgetown, Kentucky

Leaving Tracks:
A Prairie Guide

Copyright © 2017 by Sarah Fawn Montgomery
ISBN 978-1-63534-082-2 First Edition
All rights reserved under International and Pan-American Copyright Conventions.
No part of this book may be reproduced in any manner whatsoever without written permission from the publisher, except in the case of brief quotations embodied in critical articles and reviews.

ACKNOWLEDGMENTS

Poems from this chapbook have appeared or are forthcoming in *Terrain, North Dakota Quarterly, New Plains Review, Midwestern Gothic, Fourteen Hills, Briar Cliff Review, Poecology, Weber: The Contemporary West, Canary: A Literary Journal of the Environmental Crisis, Natural Bridge, Moon City Review, New Madrid, Fourth River, Shadowed: Unheard Voices Anthology, Manifest West: Serenity and Severity Anthology,* and *Trailhead: Literature for the Backcountry Anthology.*

Publisher: Leah Maines

Editor: Christen Kincaid

Cover Art: Allison Hess

Author Photo: Braydn Reynolds

Cover Design: Elizabeth Maines

Printed in the USA on acid-free paper.
Order online: www.finishinglinepress.com
        also available on amazon.com

        Author inquiries and mail orders:
        Finishing Line Press
        P. O. Box 1626
        Georgetown, Kentucky 40324
        U. S. A.

Table of Contents

Catch a Wild Thing	1
Pioneer	2
Leaving Tracks	3
Barn Swallows	4
Talking Back	6
Thunderbird	7
Drowning	8
Great Aunt	10
Excluded	11
Altar	12
A Day for Elm	13
Prairie Lessons	14
Offerings	15
Woman's Work	16
Quicksand, Missouri	17
Catching Diamonds	18
Where the West Begins	19
Goodbye Yellow Brick Road	20
Murmuration	22
The Lake	23
Firefly	25
Family Heirlooms	26
Grass Roots	28

For Carson, my very own wild thing.

Catch a Wild Thing

Catch a wild thing and hold it to your heart, tail thrashing,
teeth gnashing, limbs rigid in resistance to your touch,
your attempt to make human that which is joyously not,
to connect carnivorous, bit of blood around the gums,
feces and earth buried under nails like a dirty moon.

Catch a wild thing and hold it to your heart, its back sturdy
against your chest for a fleeting moment, rib to rib,
one long arc cradling another, arms wrapped around
its body like an embrace, a caress, a chokehold,
hand cupping full around its chest so heart pumps into palm.

Catch a wild thing and hold it to your heart, smell fear
and frustration, grass; smell wood and piss, the rain
from last week and the cling of humidity to hair;
on the back of the neck smell dried wind and spit, shit,
the scent of mating, pungent and stinking and familiar.

Catch a wild thing and hold it to your heart—breathe—
your normal rhythm disrupted by its racing pulse, aflutter
like there's something more to this life than the pace
you creep at, like the only way to live here is with ferocity
and a flailing for survival, all teeth and claw and genitals.

Catch a wild thing and hold it to your heart late at night
in the dark domed by stars, you a small thing too,
in that abyss, contained by an arc, heaving and sweaty,
heart ablaze in that stillness as you wrestle with the wild,
with yourself, fighting for a place in the here and now.

Pioneer

To lay down roots on the plains, try
to make something so untamed your own,
is to move closer, only a membrane of grass
separating you from the thrum that pumps beneath,
a tempting position what with
the horizon stretched before your gaze
like the back of a lover, naked and exposed.

But intimacy with this place is difficult,
the resistance of the flesh below
your weight, your work, your will.
Plow, pull from the earth your desire,
each season always the wild storms,
the slow build and danger, the release,
rush and sweet seeping after,
all moist and heaving green.

Trace the smooth thigh of the river,
your hand on the rounded belly of a hill—
suddenly the brittle bone, the spine
of the Rockies buckling and rising,
the dense weather that divide brings,
cackling lightning, rough winds,
the temperament towards destruction,
a permanent wilderness
despite all your best intentions.

Leaving Tracks
    —after Don Gayton

When Daddy's cement is sticky
he holds my wrists in his calloused hands
and presses my palms to leave a mark.

We are leaving impressions, he says,
to make sure the shape will hold.

He's got my name, too, carved blocked
into the split posts holding up the line
between our farm and the prairie margin.

We make these marks, Daddy says,
so we remember how to get back home.

It's like the slashes through these Dakotas—
great sweeps along ridges and river valleys,
trails where the buffalo walked heavy,

pushed their shaggy shoulders into the rock,
left their palms long across the land.

The Barn Swallows
—after Ted Kooser

*The barn swallows are leaving
early this year,* he says,
the old poet, the leathered farmer
who has spent seventy seasons
on the Nebraska plains,
laying rhyme and seed
in metrical, mathematical precision,
saving nails and old pipe in case,
a bit of flannel and a leaky kettle,
driving the same dirt road
until he knows the temperament
of the gears and the gravel,
the winter's cruel wind and glorious ice,
the way the world numbs, unconcerned
during the cold season of happenstance,
then the sudden sleight of hand of spring,
rabbits and snakes in the grass,
the fleeting fair-weather month
before the heavy heat of summer,
the way it hangs about a man's body
while he replaces shingles
or moves an outhouse across the yard,
before writing a line, a short stanza,
sipping coffee at the edge of a morning,
the edge of a pond, the edge of a season,
fall's crisp reminder warning of winter.

*The barn swallows are leaving
early this year*, he repeats,
thumbing through his memory
and the little books of verse
he's kept over the seasons of his lifetime.
He manages this early migration
by blanketing the windows of his farmhouse,

picking fruit from the heavy apple tree,
watching for the first pheasant hunters,
settling down in his old armchair
with his almanac and dog, a pen,
eyes to the soft undersides
of the determined birds above.

Talking Back

When Mama says the word is final,
pulls her lips into a flat, thin line
like a fault, plates grating, erupting temper,
she says, "Because I said so,"
and it means no more back talking,
and the argument is dead
like the electrocuted cow we saw
on the prairie after a thunderstorm,
eyes glossy, tongue silent and frothy,
or the deer on the side of the road
crushed under the wheels of some kid
that didn't listen to his wise Daddy
and drove too fast on a Friday night.
Mama crosses her arms, kills the request,
or the question, or the earnest plea,
and goes back to canning peaches
or shelling peas, snapping them clean
with her strong, calloused hands.
She turns her back and opens the oven,
yeast and steam hitting us hot in the face.
No one says a word—we know it's done—
but we can't help but think of when Mama
lops the head off a clean white chicken,
tries to silence it with a single slice,
and it runs the yard a while anyway
spurting blood and flapping.
Or the snakes we spy in dusty fields,
the ones Mama slices with her sharp hoe,
whacking their long bodies right in two,
hushing their hiss, their rattle, protest, nag.
Except she can't turn her back on the bodies,
because even snakes freshly killed can sass,
and the dying and dead still possess the reflex
to open wide and—like a mouthy child—bite
one last time, venomous at the shush.

Thunderbird

A storm must be more
than a gathering of clouds,
wind and premonition,
eyes to the skies outside,
the smell of copper and nickel
taste of green air and fear,
more than great gusts of wind,
gashes of light through the night,
instead a Thunderbird—
dark, wild thing with everlasting wings
spreading out across the Plains,
talons and brittle beak piercing
the sky to let through the rain,
sharp cry rolling thunder,
fields cowering below,
eyes bright where the light
stabs through the cloud cover,
jagged heat crackling, scorching,
warning people that this creature
whips wind with its wings
and if so inclined, so temperamental,
can cause a brutal storm, fire and flood,
tornado or torrential snow,
flights of ice, all fierce and fantastic,
yet always with the promise
of something fragrant, something green
underground and growing upward,
the quiet touch of renewal.

Drowning

When the neighbor kid got sick,
that summer of all the storms—
chaos in the altitude,
cicadas screeching for cover,
birds flying clean into the sides of barns,
sky growing green
to the tune of tornado sirens—
and all that heavy, oppressive heat,
folks said it was the ecstasy
he must have been taking on the tractor,
watching the wheat spread out in waves
of kaleidoscopic colors, light echoing
off of the big plains sky,
making stained glass of his vision.

The temperatures that summer
drove others to madness,
girls taking off their tops at the pool,
Mrs. Jones running for the ice cream truck,
robe open and big breasts flapping,
and one sweltering Sunday morning
the preacher so fed up with flies
he muttered, "Holy Hell,"
and dismissed the congregation early.
Still, the neighbor kid sat under the sun
plowing field after field all August,
a damp spot bleeding down his back.

Eventually he started seeing things
he said, when he came inside
for a drink and to wipe the dust
away from the back of his burned neck,
and he developed a habit of watching
from the edges of his eyes,
baring his strong teeth back
like a skittish horse.
Must be the drugs, folks insisted,
and his parents soon agreed,
what with the way they saw him rock
on the tractor lately, as if he were sick.

Another storm was coming that day,
clouds creeping in all afternoon,
making the light play tricks,
and perhaps that's why he saw
an ocean in the fields of oats and flax,
a great rippling body of water—
and a sea it had been once,
his grandfather plowing up
the fossil of an ocean creature.
At the first lightning crack
he dove, flinging his body
into the path the tractor was carving,
the machine simply sailing over the swell,
the rain falling anyway, unconcerned.

Great Aunt

Words bone sharp and raging from a ragged jaw on a sagged porch. A woman patched in scraps, yellow calloused fingers dangling chained cigarettes, spiral whipping quicktime around her hurricane mouth on a slow afternoon. Broken bike, dirty dog, rusted can. Worn down from a man, or another baby or a town, frowning when downing a hot beer—tastes like piss—hip cocked, eyes squinting at the sun, no fear of the future because it can't get much worse. Shooing away flies crowded around a sweaty face like shit, spatting out words like clotted blood or something on fire, like gunmetal.

Excluded

> —*The 1989 Rand McNally World Atlas chose to exclude parts of North Dakota, South Dakota, and Oklahoma based on an "editorial decision."*

Because all there is to see
in South Dakota are the monuments
built to men in stone,
their likenesses permanently etched
by the force of dynamite,
mankind all the better for it.
There are the four faces
polished shining and white,
stoic over the Black Hills.
Drive a few minutes over to see
the impressive face of a man
who will one day ride his horse
to become a world record.
The Badlands are there too,
their strata like a layer cake.
For a fee, the kids can war whoop
at a few dozen Indian pit stops,
the burden of privilege lifted
because their parents paid
for authentic souvenirs.
A few major cities—
the capital, for instance,
and the places visible by freeway—
are included, and the waterways,
which give the maps a bit of color.
No matter the texture—
small towns and rundown farms.
Follow this map and the roads give out,
scale suddenly inaccurate,
the sense of here and now confused,
tied up with when and where
back on page eight.
End up lost between horizon and sky,
in the marrow of this place,
the very reason to come at all.

Altar

If Yosemite is a cathedral,
peaks like spires, highest point devotion
to a force worthy of the incline,
the mountain nave lengthening
to contain those who come to pray,
and the Grand Canyon is full of temples,
sacred spaces made in and of the rock,
worship for the strata of the place,
the depth of our impermanence,
then the Plains are an altar,
a flatness for sacrifice—
winters of isolation, of ice, of hunger,
the shimmer of mirage in the summer,
green skies sickly like premonition,
a funnel forming in the distance,
years bent at the plow for wheat, for corn,
body broken by the work of generations.
They are a great space on which to lay offerings—
a rock rubbed smooth by the bison,
the feather of a barn swallow, cicada husk,
long grass gone crisp in the sun,
crabapples, chokecherries—
our compulsion to pray fed
by the vastness of sky and space
the smell of fragrant smoke,
fields afire for thousands of years,
blazing the way to rebirth.

A Day for Elm
—after Donald Hall

Today is a day for elm,
which heats the stove steadily,
like the warm beat from your chest,
reliable as an old lover's hand,
the way it remembers the body's bends,
the best and broken parts of your life.
With eight inches of snow expected
and nowhere to be, today is also a day
for hound dogs and heavy quilts,
and that lazy, longing way of gazing
out the window at the world
gone soft and still in just an hour.

Not every day is a day for elm:
some days require the kettle
at the ready—hardwoods like oak
heating the house slowly—gleaming
metal hissing the boiling point's arrival.
And some days, when the oven is full
of bread, yeast and steam seeping out
when the iron door is cracked open,
or the sweetness of sugared plum pie,
are meant for ash—not the remnants
of fire, but the easy way the wood blazes,
makes things rise, able to sustain.

Prairie Lessons
    —Found from Paul Gruchow's "What the Prairie Teaches Us."

Meet every natural contingency,
There need be no contradiction between utility and beauty.
Poised to exploit,
Put down deep roots first.
Do not flower without the nourishment to make good seed.
Be competitive without also being destructive.
Frequently fall short—
Work that matters doesn't always show.
Consider the uses that may be made of our setbacks.
Flourish in a hard place.

Offerings

This place makes us leave bits of ourselves behind—
the years of our youth, a finger in the combine, even the farm
when the crops won't yield, abandoned house overtaken
by the wildness it was meant to settle, prairie grass
and the trees moving in, holding things upright.

A hardening happens here, work and weather making us
tough and brittle like cicadas, giving us all we can handle
until we are just a shell. When we think we've had enough
we squeeze from the husk and fly somewhere else,
always returning to chirp the same song with the others.

Perhaps the Plains have earned it, the years, the house,
our brittle bodies. These are our hard offerings to a hard place.
But we survive, however marked. There are more years.
The house still stands. And up close, the fallen skeletons
are delicate, glowing amber and translucent.

Woman's Work

Mend the tablecloth after the clean supper dishes are away in the cupboards lined with fresh paper. Be sure to finish sewing so you can set out breakfast the next morning, the strong coffee and the biscuits, the sausage you made, casings slick between your fingers like when you deliver a calf, reach into the darkness, pulling the creature toward release, clutching the wet afterbirth. Dress the children, the clothes you made last spring already tightening around their burgeoning limbs. Note the hem coming down. ABCs. 123s. Recite while you wipe down after breakfast. Lead your brood up and down the cellar stairs, stacking the jars of peaches you assembled last Saturday, children sucking at their fingers all afternoon, faces sticky with syrup. Skip the wobbly second step, grateful there's no storm this time, no need for sternness as you herd the small ones inside, eventually feigning softness, singing to distract their cries at the dervish overhead. Remember to repair the step. Make tomato juice to go with lunch sandwiches, squeezing the fruit you twist from the vine until pulpy, straining it smooth. Wash dishes. Wipe down table. With your pail head past the field you plow, know the length and lean of, the few dips and divots. Spend the afternoon bent in the sun towards raspberries, huckleberries, wild blueberries, armpits and fingers stained with the work, prickles bouncing off the callouses, hardened hands smoothing out a pie crust. Kill, pluck, fry a chicken for dinner. Remind the children not to cry—there is no time for tears, for fears, even for aches and pains. Wipe down the table after clean supper dishes are away in the cupboards lined with fresh paper. Think about breakfast, the strong coffee, the eggs you'll need to fetch, the juice yet to be squeezed as you piece together the elk skins left from the hunt, the meat long cooked or frozen away for winter. Sew long into night, skin all that remains of what was, flesh worked down to nothing.

Quicksand, Missouri

Inside the curve of the river,
where water rests against the bank
like lovers spooning close,
seems the best spot for fishing,
a sandbar like a beach,
like you could use the shore
under your feet to push off
in a boat or set yourself down
in an inner tube, beer on your belly,
drifting by Saturday and the world,
fishermen standing and waving,
casting long into the flow,
closing their eyes while the bait
bobs and bounces, slow dervish
with the eddying ripples.

Watch out, local folks warn real slow,
like they're chewing something strong.
That sand's jelly. Sand's slurry.
And they tell of how once a boy
No more'n eight waded out fishing,
his grandpa watching behind.
He thought it was firm, they say,
but the boy got caught in the quiver,
that place where the saturation
meets the flow, that thin between
separating skin and muscle,
the cushion between skull and brain,
right and wrong, dream and awake,
next-to-nothing between nostalgia, now.

Catching Diamonds

First, tiptoe through grass
careful to avoid the dew
nighttime makes around your gown,
the one you wear to try and sleep,
pink tattered lace around the hem.

Second, take a canning jar
in one hand, cup the lid
in the other while twirling—
head up, eyes pinched shut—
so quick your little girl
skirt flares full in the moon.

Next, slow down the spin to listen
to the sound of night noises—
frog vibration, violin cicada screech,
Mama trying to cry silently in the bathroom,
Daddy cracking open a beer, slasher scream on TV.
Open your eyes to watch the world
rotate, the slow blink of lightning
bugs dancing in the dark.

Then stop, pounce about the yard
after the flicker, around the big tree
as you try to catch the gleam
of a dozen floating diamonds.
Capture one at last in your glass—
a homemade lantern in your Kansas kingdom.

Finally, grasp the small thing
between your smaller painted nails
—watch it flutter fairylike—
then prick off the head to claim
the center, a jewel for your ring.

Where the West Begins

There's a place where the prairie—that flat expanse
of wheat and corn, that place where you forget
your feet on the ground, the rhythm of your step,
and focus instead on the big bowl of sky overturned
above you, the way it cups your existence
as far as you can see, farther than you fathom,
farther still, the way the world orients to it,
crops turned to light that lasts late into night,
ten o'clock summers and not dark yet,
rain and the way a storm comes quickly,
darkens the air though it's still warm out,
the way the wind can knock you clean over,
can whip into a dervish, pull things into its core—
gives way, margins out and begins to roll over and under
itself like a sleeping bag or hay in the fall,
where topography rises up like braille
to make myths of the land readable, to tell
tales of the West, where it becomes rough,
more sudden than expected, mountains in range,
and you realize you've moved your eyes from the skies
like the gophers you see in spring, the rabbits in winter
outside their holes, staring up amazed at the world,
and you're left instead gasping at craggy peaks,
ragged and blue and purple in the light, hard.
The place where the West begins begins to change you,
and you focus on how to succeed, overcome,
how to move up and over these mountains,
trample their strength with your will.
How to march Westward—Manifest Destiny—
the world not resting under the sky as before,
instead now cowering under your foot.

Goodbye Yellow Brick Road

> *"You can't plant me in your penthouse. I'm going back to my plow."*
> –Elton John

We know that path means fame
or fortune, or more importantly,
that shoot-for-the-sky lie
we believe in the inevitable high
of our rosy youth—
you know, the one about the blaze
your star will leave across
what could have been darkness.

But Elton knows not to believe
that desperate recycled promise,
knows it most likely won't happen,
folks dreaming with their mouths open
until their longing is left dry and brittle.

Or maybe it will, and you'll leave
Kansas, or Iowa, or Missouri—
Misery, folks say like no one's
ever heard that one before—
and you'll hitch a ride to L.A.,
some old man's weathered hand
weighing down your knee.

You'll get there starving,
and eat a burger and onion rings,
look around at the town unable to see
stars or the Hollywood sign—unable to see shit—
for the smog and façade,

When folks back home sing along
they clench the steering wheel
as they stare out at the fields,
and then they lean back, close their eyes,
because that's what you do with the blues.
They wail, "Ahh Ahh Ahh,"
all moan and sigh, a hint
of that dream still desperate
to crawl out their clenched throats.

Maybe you aren't there yet—
where home means retreat, defeat—
because you swear old Elton is crooning:
I'm going back to my cloud.
Sure you hitched yourself back,
sure you're sitting plowside,
blades chewing up roots,
but you're leaning back in the sun,
still looking up, still thinking sky.

Murmuration

Today the frost on the windshield is barely there,
like tiny bird footprints, dainty and forked,
or the V's of flight in a child's drawing.
I don't scrape the ice, just ease onto the busy street,
flashes of a hundred headlights stark
against the glittering morning as folks rush
to work, hunched against their steering wheels,
and the cold, and the dull of Monday morning.

I pause at a crowded intersection, cars stopped
as people avoid eye contact and wait their turn
to turn away from one another. The frost figures
on the glass float over my sight as I turn the car.

They look like a murmuration—a thousand starlings
synchronized in the sky, undulating waves like a scarf
above the Plains, coming together and swaying apart,
soft like wheat or sorghum until the mass moves
overhead and the rapid rustle of wings reveals
the force it takes to keep this thing precise, pristine,
moving on a dime, a collective body, warm and beating,
each knowing in an instant where the other is going.

We move as one—the bird-ice and me—rhythmic,
turning together like dance, waltzing through town
until the crystals begin to melt, muddy the window,
and I arrive at work, stop the car, leave them to the sun.

The Lake

The lake came with little warning,
just a town meeting announcing
This land's for public use now
and a map of what the water
would look like when the houses went.

No one protested much
because what could you do
when it came down to recreation
and the finer points of city planning?

The Johnsons were long-timers,
so they sold for a tidy profit,
and the Smiths had wanted to downsize
ever since their son went off to State,
and they got inspired to up and move
to sunny Florida and bigger water.

But Widow Brown wouldn't leave,
kept on gardening like she never heard,
ignoring the signs around town
advertising a new swimming spot,
a dock for shiny motorboats,
and even a summer stand for dipped cones
and dogs with different kinds of mustard.

She disregarded the men in hardhats
and the government paperwork insisting
no one was really asking for permission.
She'd return from grocery shopping
to caution tape around the yard and tractors
alongside her old wheelbarrow and spade.

Eventually they busted the windows and pipes
so she couldn't stay, and built up the land
around her yellow house, pumping the basin
full of water like a backyard mud hole.

Swim deep enough, past legs and rafts,
or the bottoms of those shiny boats,
and you'll see her overturned barrow,
shards of window like a shark's teeth.

Fish swim in and out of the opening,
circling the living room,
walls gone green with algae,
finding themselves at the table
the widow left carefully set for tea.

Firefly

A firefly is a runner's shortness of breath on a dust trail at dusk; the pulse of your electric heart, big as two fighting fists; a darkened kiss on a footbridge, flickering off the water more than burning, churning stars; a winking premonition; a slow-motion reminder of what remains unseen; a firework's fierce flash in the sky, shimmering silent pyrotechnic polyphaga; lightning like its nickname, atmospheric electrostatic charge, white veins illuminating nocturnal like spider webs and jellyfish, rivers and ribbon dancing, staccato and forked, sheeted or heated, moving with nature's unmapped method, sometimes daring to dart directly where it's just danced; the sudden shimmer of orgasm, the way it throbs long after it leaves.

Family Heirlooms

Inside hands closed like prayer
are the relics grandfather has unwrapped
from the handkerchief hidden
in an old tin tobacco box
dented but wiped clean of dust.
The seeds no bigger than a pinprick,
glossy brown teardrops,
ink dripped from the nib.
They burrow into his wrinkles
searching for soil, yearning to grow.
He holds up his palms like an offering.

These kernels straddle history,
plucked each harvest from the hardiest plants,
those that survived the harshness of seasons,
abundant despite the extremes,
stored away with the good silver,
the quilts growing thin with rot,
yellowing photos and a rusting kettle,
until the need for nostalgia,
for better times, climes, yields,
for survival compels their use.

Plant these to time travel
to grandmother's longest winter,
like the one that ended this June,
graduation indoors because of snow,
or the summer the neighbor boy
saw waves in the fields full of wheat,
went crazy from the oppressive heat,
or a famer suffocated in his grain bin
after falling in, drowned by his work,
mouth full of the crop he fought for.

The plant's memory goes further
back still, to when the railroad came,
bisected the land, travelers and strangers
halfway between coming and going,
never intending to stay: what remained
was that here is not easy, not civil,
here is nothing, really, just flyover.

Like burning the prairie to take it back
to richness, growth from the ash,
feeling a storm behind the eyes
days before it announces its arrival,
knowing which woods burn slowest,
or that swallows leave as winter comes,
or planting a dead perch next to the corn
means flowers feed from what is lost,
the seeds are a prairie lesson for survival,
a gift to those who don't give up,
move on, move West, to easier ground.

Grass Roots

Separate strands with turned out hands—
like swimming but sharper—
diving into the prairie brush. Bristle, bend.
Concentrate to isolate one from many.
Trace a finger down the length, careful
to avoid the sharp edge, slick as a blade.
Reaching ground, push pointer finger
into the soil to go further along the shaft.
Wriggle nail and knuckle, dig down,
careful not to rip the knot beneath,
coiled and so densely matted.

It takes effort now—force, stamina,
the sun on the prairie leaving skin slick—
two fingers, three, dirt rising past the wrist.
Roots beyond grasp spur curiosity,
for they hold the whole world up,
an inverted tree underground.
Forearm. The tender crook of the elbow.
When the shoulder sticks, remove
and place hands together like prayer.
Dive headfirst into the space created,
eyes closed, wriggling like a blind worm.

Feet motionless, anchored above,
try to grasp where this system stops.
Feel the root you've followed thicken,
hard, controlled, and decisive,
an enticing leash further.
Become small, surrounded, subsumed.
Toes slide from the soil perch.
There's only so much breath,
so swim fast and determined
to find the end of this world.
Deeper, darker, forever lasting.

Sarah Fawn Montgomery holds an MFA in creative nonfiction from California State University-Fresno and a PhD in creative writing from the University of Nebraska-Lincoln, where she teaches and works as *Prairie Schooner*'s Nonfiction Assistant Editor. She is the author of *The Astronaut Checks His Watch* (Finishing Line Press). Her work has been listed as notable several times in *Best American Essays*, and her poetry and prose have appeared in various magazines including *Confrontation, Crab Orchard Review, DIAGRAM, Fugue, Georgetown Review, The Los Angeles Review, Natural Bridge, Nimrod, North Dakota Quarterly, Passages North, The Pinch, Puerto del Sol, Southeast Review, The Rumpus, Terrain, Zone 3* and others.

www.ingramcontent.com/pod-product-compliance
Lightning Source LLC
LaVergne TN
LVHW041512070426
835507LV00012B/1517